Divine Love
Henry Fernandez

Foreword by Bishop Earl Paulk

6/21/98

Divine Love
by Henry Fernandez

Copyright ©1998 Henry Fernandez
All rights reserved. This book is protected under the copyright laws of the United States of America. This book may not be copied or reprinted for commercial gain or profit. The use of short quotations or occasional page copying for personal or group study is permitted and encouraged. Permission will be granted upon request. Unless otherwise identified, Scripture quotations are from the King James Version of the Bible.

ISBN 1-58169-006-1
For Worldwide Distribution
Printed in the U.S.A.

Companion Press
An Imprint of Genesis Communications, Inc.
P.O. Box 91011 • Mobile, AL 36691
(888) 670-7463
Email: GenesisCom@aol.com

DEDICATION

This book is lovingly dedicated to my wife Carol, whose support and unfailing love has stimulated the seeds of greatness in my life.

To Archbishop Earl Paulk, for his wisdom and counseling.

To my father and mother, who gave me the basic training in the Word of God.

To the executive board and ministers of Plantation Worship Center Ministries.

To all the members and partners of PWCM around the world.

TABLE OF CONTENTS

Foreword..v

1. Human Love Versus Divine Love...1
2. If You Would Be Perfect..12
3. Forgiveness Transforms..26
4. Leave It Behind..40
5. Onward and Upward..48

FOREWORD

The word *love* is probably the most ambiguous word in any language. It can apply to a brief feeling, an emotion, care for an animal, some kind of apparel, a romantic feeling and a lifelong relationship. Yet none of these descriptions matches the definition given in God's Word known as *agape* love. It is so easy for one to say, "I love that car," or "I love that house," without having any connection whatsoever toward the meaning of love referred to in God's Word.

The love that is called divine also carries with it the connotation of *redemption*. It is a love that asks *nothing* in return. It is also a love that produces a positive response in the person upon whom it is bestowed. This is the kind of love that reaches out to the unlovable—those who try to reject it. The kind of love referred to in I Corinthians 13 suggests the right attitude, the right motive and the right action we are to take if we would reach for the heights. We are to love because that is what God wants, and we want to be like Him.

An interesting story in the Bible describes this kind of surpassing love to us. A rich young ruler approaches Jesus, posing the question, "Good Master, what shall I do to inherit eternal life?" Before making a response, Jesus looked at the young man—suggesting that He focused intensely upon him and discerned immediately his need. Then an interesting observation is recorded, that "Jesus loved him." His was a love that, at the moment, did not get the right response, but loved anyway. Later on, that young man must have remembered Jesus' words and his whole experience with Jesus, which was *life-changing,* whether or not he chose to respond to it. Divine love is operative regardless of the response on the part of the one being loved. We need to pray for the grace to receive it, and He will bless us beyond comprehension.

"God so loved the world that He gave His only begotten Son" (John 3:16). God loves infinitely, absolutely, without condition or restriction. His love does not wait to see if there will be a response to it. *"While we were yet in sin, Christ died for us"* (Romans 5:8). God's love is measured only by that which flows out of us with a desire to give. The impartation of His love to us brings about divine results.

In Galatians 5:6, we learn that what is beneficial is the faith that works by love:

> *For in Jesus Christ neither circumcision availeth anything, nor uncircumcision; but faith which worketh by love.*

For faith to be operative, it must be based on love. If this is so, God's love operative in us must far exceed what we are capable of by human love alone. In divine love, faith operates to impart the power of God, who alone can produce redemptive results. Therefore, repeated often in the Gospels are expressions such as, "And Jesus, moved with compassion, healed them all" (Matthew 14:14). His love knew no end and never tired but gave until all were satisfied. Whether it was a blind beggar or the woman with an issue of blood, all the miracles Jesus accomplished were performed because Jesus loved people.

True laborers in the harvest fields of God must love with this unceasing love. Only this kind of compassion produces the response that enlists people in the work of the kingdom. Look again at where Jesus, moved with compassion, called for laborers to minister to scattered sheep (Matthew 9:36-38). Only divine love takes us out of our comfort zone and causes us to go into the regions beyond—to what Shakespeare calls "the undiscover'd country . . . (that) makes us bear the ills we have than fly to others we know not of" (*Hamlet,* Act III, scene i, 56). We are to love those God gives us without reserve.

Some of us are called to love those He has given us who are not of our own background, because He sends us to love them.

How many times have we read stories of missionaries going into regions of the earth and literally giving their lives for people they have not known before? The love that cares enough to die for who and what it believes in can only be called divine.

Think for a moment how many families would be saved if parents displayed divine love and care. There would be no abused children who cry themselves to sleep at night nor rebellious teenagers to terrorize society. The kind of love that flows from the divine heart of God takes the sword out of the hand of the enemy.

True ministers of God must operate out of divine love if they expect redemptive results. This love does not just reach out to those in the congregation who can give support or approval, but also to those who have lost their way in life. His love takes away the limpness, blindness, deafness and hopelessness and replaces those limitations with a confidence rooted in eternal love.

It is noteworthy that different Greek words are used to express divine love (*agape*) and human love (*filio* and *eros*). We should take time to be sure that we are moving in God's love and not in some merely human imitation. If we do love as He loves, the result will be the salvation of an otherwise hopeless world.

The greatest expression of divine love through a human being was effected by Jesus as He hung upon the cross and said, *"Father, forgive them for they know not what they do"* (Luke 23:34). His unconditional gift of self is love lifted to its highest expression. Perfect love accomplishes what it sets out to do—drawing all men unto Himself (John 12:32). Oh, that we may seek God's divine love so that we may carry on the exalted mission for which He died!

—Bishop Earl Paulk

Chapter One
Human Love Versus Divine Love

Incline your ear, and come unto me: hear, and your soul shall live; and I will make an everlasting covenant with you, even the sure mercies of David. . . . Seek the Lord while he may be found, call ye upon him while he is near: Let the wicked forsake his way, and the unrighteous man his thoughts: and let him return unto the LORD, and he will have mercy upon him; and to our God, for he will abundantly pardon. For my thoughts are not your thoughts, neither are your ways my ways, saith the LORD. For as the heavens are higher than the earth, so are my ways higher than your ways, and my thoughts than your thoughts (Isaiah 55:3,6-9).

Our human love is limited by many conditions. We choose who is worthy of our love and measure out our love accordingly. We also set limits, consciously and unconsciously, as to how much difficulty we can handle in our relationships. We come to the end of our ability rather quickly at times, so much so that some of us have come to the conclusion that we need a heart transplant: we need God's divine heart in order to love His people as *He* loves them.

Our hearts need to be filled with His unending love. The gentle healing touch of the Savior is the only thing capable of redeeming all the situations in our lives which cause us to lose heart. His divine love indeed transforms the way we see other human beings: our enemies become our brothers and sisters.

God gives us the grace to value each other as children of the same God. He gives us His ability to love in a way that gives abundant life to all, and even the seemingly unlovable—those who appear to have no redeeming qualities whatsoever. We must seek to imitate the Master, who spared nothing of Himself in His total offering of Himself to His Father. When we surrender every bit of resistance to God's power at work in our lives, the irresistible attraction of perfect love, we will receive an outpouring of blessings we have never known before, and will find the happiness and peace we have always hoped to enjoy.

Love Thy Neighbor

From personal experience, I can tell you that God wants us to live out what we preach, so that our words will be meaningful, with the power to reach people in such a way that their capacity to love is increased and their lives transformed.

I met my wife Carol over 15 years ago. We both went to the same church in Brooklyn, New York, professing to be Christians who loved the Lord. However, my first impression of Carol was not favorable: she seemed self-centered and power-driven. It was very difficult for me to relate to her because I resented people who thought they were in any way special or deserved to be treated differently by everyone else. Carol was very confident in herself, which made it hard for me to deal with her. We were different in many ways, and as time went by, began to hate each other.

After a few weeks had passed by, our pastor unexpectedly appointed Carol to be the teacher of our Sunday School teenage class (ages 13-16) and asked me to be her assistant. I was upset at being forced to be in close contact with her—something I absolutely did not want. We decided that the best way to keep the peace was to teach alternating Sundays.

It so happened that the first lesson I was to teach, taken from John 13:35, was titled "Love Thy Neighbor" and read as follows, *"By this shall all men know that ye are my disciples, if ye have love one to another."* This word from God was just like a knife piercing my heart, because there I was—doing everything to justify that I was a Christian—and still falling short of my calling as a disciple.

I had grown up in a Holiness Pentecostal church and was

taught the difference between right and wrong. In my mind, I felt that if I went to church and gave my time and talents to God, He would honor my efforts as the best that I could do. I felt so right and perfect until that day when God confronted me. He revealed something personal to me when He said, "Are you my disciple? And if you *are,* you must have love for one another."

Even though I was still dealing with the conviction His word brought, I decided to teach the class. During class, a student asked me, "How can you handle family members who think they are better than others?" Stunned by her question, I asked her to explain what she meant. The girl replied that her sister believed that she was "God's gift to the world." Her sister criticized everything she did, so much so that she couldn't bear to be around her. She tried to love her sister but found it nearly impossible. She asked me what I would do in her situation. I began to believe that God was setting me up. . . .

For obvious reasons, though, I decided to evade her question. So God had another student ask me the same question in a different way. I was trapped: how was I to honestly answer their questions without sending out a contradictory message—one different from what I was living out? I wanted to say that if you do not like a person, you can ignore that person and move on. But 19 students were staring at me, and I didn't want to offend Carol, the teacher in charge, who was present at the time!

After a moment of hesitation, I chose to answer the question biblically. I said that when we find it difficult to love someone, we should pray, asking God to help us love that person. I quoted John 3:16, which says, *"For God so loved the world that He gave His only begotten Son that whosoever believeth in Him should not perish but have everlasting life."* I told them that God loves us and blesses us regardless of who we are. God doesn't love only those who are a joy to be around; He loves "whosoever"—meaning everyone. He extends His unlimited love to everyone, regardless of whether they are aware of His love, want it, or reject it. Whether we are good or not so good, God loves us.

I even pointed out the passage in the Bible that says, *"If it be possible, as much as lieth in you, live peaceably with all men"* (Romans 12:18). We ought to try to understand that we were all created with different likes and dislikes but are on the same side. If God can look beyond our differences and accept us, we can do the same for our neighbors. The ground is level at the foot of the cross: we all stand beneath it in need of redemption in our daily lives.

By this time I knew that I was being hypocritical, because I was telling these students to love people whose personalities did not agree with them when I, in fact, was not doing so. We proceeded to spend the remainder of the class talking about loving each other and understanding our differences.

Throughout the class Carol said nothing, knowing I was not living what I was preaching. She might have struggled with the message just as I did, knowing how difficult it is for any one of us to forgive and love that one person who does not agree with us and "pushes our anger buttons."

When I got home I sat down in my living room and began to reflect on what took place during Sunday school. God inspired me to plan on doing the things I advised the little girl to do. I would try to find the positive things about Carol and not the negative. Not long after this decision, we began communicating more and understanding each other better.

Communicating played a vital part in our understanding each other; it even opened the door to fellowship. Once God removed the way I saw Carol, I was able to look at her *as God sees her*. We were able to go shopping together, go to church together and call each other on the telephone—talking for hours. Never in my wildest dreams did I think I would be going out with a woman whom I had at first resented.

As time went by, I began to notice how much I enjoyed being around her! More and more, I found myself unable to sleep until I talked to her (I wonder why). I came to know her well and started loving her for who she was as a person. Believe it or not, I was falling in love with the person whom I had serious personality conflicts with; and it was only at this time that I came to know that she was the very one who could understand me best and love me for who I am.

I asked myself, "What caused this hate to turn to love?" The Holy Spirit revealed to me that the moment I started loving Carol on the basis of John 13:35, divine love began to operate in my life. In the past, I was looking at her with eyes of the flesh—through my feelings—which can be misleading.

God wants us to love people through His love, unconditionally—through Him, with Him and in Him, in the power of unity that comes from the Holy Spirit. This spiritual power to love can assist us in every relationship, in every difficulty: at church, at home, with friends, business associates, while traveling, moving, etc.

In the Name of Love

There are several different meanings of the word *love* in the world. People say they love, but the actions that arise from out of that love are far different from what we'd expect. They will say that they love you, but if you wrong them, they will kill you. People actually kill in the name of love. People will say that they love you, and if they are double-minded, they will turn around and stab you in the back. People will act as if they like you, but criticize you in order to destroy your character. But is that true love—what Jesus wants for His disciples?

We must distinguish God's love from the many variants of human love that all too often take their place in our hearts, causing disaster in our lives. There are some serious misconceptions about love today; it has even been confused with abuse—the twisted idea that it has to hurt in order to be felt—but this is not love. This all too common problem (and others like it) proves the need for divine love as the only solution to the complex problems in life.

A Love Beyond Compare

The word divine means "of God, coming from God and having the nature of God." Our love is based on what we see externally and physically, and is therefore limited to the good we can perceive in another—as opposed to what is really there. We choose who we like according to our tastes and our concept of an ideal companion. We think about how loving another will benefit us: what they are going to give us: praise, pleasure, meals, clothes, jewelry, vacations; how they make us feel, etc.

Honestly, many of us base our love on what others can do for us; and if they fulfill our expectations, we will love them. We try to give others what they want, with varying degrees of success or failure. "Well, if you do this for me, you're my friend," is how we view people. We do not see that the best we can attain by this way of thinking is a union of mutual self-interest and motivation. As long as others please us and we please them, there is agreement, and the relationship lasts. Repeating the vow, "For as long as you both shall *live*," does not say "For as long as you both shall *love*."

We often unconsciously base love on what others can do for us. But how many of us can truly say that we have the forgiving nature of God to love a person who hates us to the core? It takes an extraordinary person to love someone that despises who you are and what you stand for. For I Corinthians 13:1 says,

Though I speak with the tongues of men and of angels, and have not charity, I am become as sounding brass, or a tinkling cymbal.

Can you say that you love people when they deceitfully or spitefully use you, say bad things about you, or even burn your house down? We must examine both our spoken and our unspoken Christianity, including our intentions and our testimony. When we say that we love God, we must mean that we love all people and have a passion for the salvation of souls, desiring that peoples' lives change for the better as a result of God's love flowing from us.

In order to act as Jesus, with His heart of charity, we have to go beyond the level of regular, ordinary human love and truly love people for who they are—as they are. Many people in life have hurt us. We want to love them with God's love, but more often we tend to say, "Well, you hurt me; I'm writing you off my list!" Our nature is to judge those who hurt us and declare our hatred for them. Many Christians' spiritual lives have thus been stagnated, due to years of hurts experienced and the unforgiveness and built-up anger that followed. As a result, we may still be struggling with past issues everyday but only realize it when a sensitive area is touched unintentionally by others. Our inner peace is eroded, lessening our ability to relate closely with anyone.

Everyone Makes Mistakes

In order to really love, we have to understand that we all have made mistakes in our lives and take that into account when we start to judge others. Some relationships were never meant to be from the beginning. We may have walked out of the will of God or didn't know who was right for us, and entered into a relationship that took more than we could ever give. As a result, we made large errors in our choices from the beginning, and our relationship ended badly. Does that mean that God will not make a way for us? No, all you need to do is pick up where you left off by putting that behind you.

We have allowed people to dictate to us how to live; we have given them—and the enemy—a *power* over us they should not have. Because this person didn't treat you right—messed up your life—you might think for the rest of your life that you're never going to come out victorious! We should not "hop from one person to the next," searching for a perfect human being with all the solutions to our problems. But we ought to confess our sins to our Advocate who intercedes for us and forgives us, and He will get us back on track—put us where we need to be and show us how we are to love. In I John 2:1-2, it is written,

> *My little children, these things write I unto you, that ye sin not. And if any man sin, we have an advocate with the Father, Jesus Christ the righteous: And he is the propitiation for our sins: and not for ours only, but also for the sins of the whole world.*

The Enemy Is The Accuser

You can go to Jesus anytime. Even if you are unable to pray, just go sit in a quiet place for long enough and you'll get the peace you need to continue. He will let you experience His presence and may give you the knowledge of what you are to do in your situation. You can say to God, "Lord, I've sinned, I've made some big errors, and I've walked out of your will—now teach me your ways!" Be concerned with your own part, and leave others to God; that is the only way to live in peace and continue loving.

God will never walk up to you, point his finger at you and say, "Remember what you did five years ago? I can't believe you did that!" He never reminds you of the sins you have left behind. In total contrast, God forgives and forgets everyone's sins:

> *And they shall teach no more every man his neighbor, and every man his brother, saying, Know the Lord: for they shall all know me, from the least of them unto the greatest of them, saith the Lord: for I will forgive their iniquity, and I will remember their sin no more* (Jeremiah 31:34).

By refusing to take offense when others come at us, we can show them how they are supposed to act, and what their attitudes toward their neighbor should be.

Love Covers a Multitude of Sins

We should remember that our sins are covered by the blood of Jesus. There was a time when we didn't know better, and there's always more for us to learn in serving God. We must realize that others have to come to the truth—God Himself will show them. We can't speed their journey by catching them up to where they need to be as quickly as we'd like. They must come to it themselves, but we *can* provide a good example. We can go to Him and cry out, "Abba Father," sincere in our repentance and desire to make amends. God will hear your cry for His divine love to renew you and recreate in you a clean heart. Divine love has to come from Him; we do not have it in ourselves. How comforting it is to think that we don't have to do anything, but can tap into the source of unlimited love. Nothing is impossible with God, not even purifying and strengthening our love for one another.

Charity Begins At Home

What kind of love do we show our family? The home is the area that the enemy is attacking more than anything else. If our lives and the love that we express are to be real, we cannot sugarcoat our Christianity: we can't just come to church, praise God, "get happy," and neglect to address difficulties at home. This ingredient of reality is what is lacking and messing up the Church. We don't know how to fix home first, where charity *ought* to begin. So instead, we try to fix the Church first and the home later, and as a result, become unbalanced. How can we preach family values to the world and not live them? Consider the personal qualifications Paul gave to Timothy for being a good deacon:

> *Likewise* must *the deacons* be *grave, not double-tongued, not given to much wine, not greedy of filthy lucre; Holding the mystery of the faith in a pure conscience. And let these also first be proved; then let them use the office of a deacon, being* found *blameless. Even so* must their *wives* be *grave, not slanderers, sober, faithful in all things. Let the deacons be the husbands of one wife, ruling their children and their own houses well. For they that have used the office of a deacon well purchase to themselves a good degree, and great boldness in the faith which is in Christ Jesus* (I Timothy 3:8-13).

He said that man must rule his house first, before he can fix the house of God. That is to say, before you can ever be qualified for leadership in the Body of Christ, start fixing your home first. Get love back into your family. It is a shame that we come to church and embrace our brothers and sisters in the Lord with such affection (they who don't have to live with us are easier to love) and yet husbands and wives will go home and relate distantly, without intimacy. Babies (and adults) need to be held and touched or they will feel unwanted.

We unthinkingly say at times, "Don't bother me; I'm going to bed." But if we ask to be left alone, we may very well be, even more than we would like. But if we are to grow, we must love despite how we are feeling. The Body of Christ is hurting because we don't have divine love in the home.

Is Human Love Enough?

Not knowing there is a divine river of power to increase the quality of our love for each other, we try to hash it out on our own. What we have may be referred to as "heart love"—whatever we feel in the heart, we express it, come what may! At its worst, it means, "You hurt me, and I'll pay you back." Many of us choose to vent our frustrations on those we trust, who are committed to love us, particularly our spouse. This expression takes place verbally and non-verbally, and its impact is felt in the home, especially if the problem is not quickly resolved. Some of us can find ourselves not speaking to our spouse for days. The silent distance can subtly edge its way into our relationship and divide us.

What Is Impossible to Man

The love we are to have for each other is to mirror the love that Jesus has for His bride, the Church, just as the Word says in Ephesians 5:25, "He gave himself up for her." In the course of our lives, God makes His love for us so real that we cannot remain unaware of it; He *will* make Himself known to us. Because we have first received His love, we are commissioned to love our neighbors. "Love thy neighbor" is a command, not an option. How, then, do we get around it? Love your friends, hate your enemies (c.f. Matthew 5:43) no longer applies. Instead of loving only those who love us, we are called to:

Love your enemies, bless them that curse you, do good to them that hate you, and pray for them which despitefully use you and persecute you; that ye may be the children of your Father which is in heaven (Matthew 5:44-45).

This teaching sounds impossible for a human being to do, and it *is*. We need the divine love to love our neighbor, and especially our spouse. *"This is my commandment, that ye love one another, as I have loved you"* (John 15:12). We can't talk about loving God when we can't love the one beside us, whom we *can* see. When we can't love on the earth, we can't love in the heavenlies. We need heavenly love to fill us up and purify our earthly love. God will take the charity we are already showing and take it to another level, in a real way sharing in His divine life. We are to be renewed totally, so that even our appearance changes, just like Moses when he came down from the mountain (Exodus 34:29-30) and Jesus upon His transfiguration (Matthew 17:2). The love of God can make us radiant.

For as the rain cometh down, and the snow from heaven, and returneth not thither, but watereth the earth, and maketh it bring forth and bud, that it may give seed to the sower, and bread to the eater: So shall my word be that goeth forth out of my mouth: it shall not return unto me void, but it shall accomplish that which I please, and it shall prosper in the thing whereto I sent it. For ye shall go out with joy and be led forth with peace: the mountains and the hills shall break forth before you into singing, and all the trees of the field shall clap their hands. Instead of the thorn shall come up the fir tree, and instead of the briar shall come up the myrtle tree: and it shall be to the Lord for a name, for an everlasting sign that shall not be cut off (Isaiah 55:10-13).

Chapter Two
If You Would Be Perfect

Then Jesus beholding him loved him, and said unto him, One thing thou lackest: go thy way, sell whatever thou hast, and give to the poor, and thou shalt have treasure in heaven: and come, take up the cross and follow me (Mark 10:21).

To love is a decision that means giving all that we have in favor of serving Jesus Christ. There are really only two possibilities for us: we follow Him or someone else. If we are to follow Him, we must do so wholeheartedly. We can always follow Him more closely. We need to walk where He walked, even to Calvary. Loving unconditionally is a cross we must bear, but it leads to Resurrection and eternal happiness. We *want* the treasure He has for us in heaven. When we love who we consider the least of His brethren—being patient even with the least desirable qualities in our neighbors—we are loving Him, and He will bless us abundantly for our efforts.

We are humbled when we strive to love as He loves. He asks us to be humble so that He can show the areas of our lives where, like the rich young man, we have not yet freed ourselves up from the things that hinder us from keeping up with Him in our daily walk.

United We Stand

Single folks come to church and hope to see examples of what true marriage is like. They want to be able to say, "When I get married, I want my relationship to be like that of that brother and sister in the Lord." Someone has to set the example for others to imitate. It would be encouraging to see families sitting together in church, but we know that presently this is not always the case. We must keep the family together as much we can, both in the church and at home.

It is a shame when a husband does not know when his wife leaves church, and upon returning home himself, cannot say for sure where she is. Have we gotten that far out of touch? We have to take care of this pressing personal matter first, because it has a great deal to do with our Christianity. Our faith does not consist merely in coming to church for about two hours, enjoying the service, and then neglecting to use what we have learned. Living the practical Christian life consistently is what counts. We all come up short on occasion, but we are seeking to do better. Whoever does the will of His Father is Jesus' brother, sister, and mother (Matthew 12:50). Jesus came that we, His family, would build up "community" in abundance:

> *The thief cometh not, but for to steal, and to kill, and to destroy: I am come that they might have life, and that they might have it more abundantly* (John 10:10).

It's Commitment

Even if one or both of you may have lost your figure or physique, your love must still endure. Our love ought to grow with time and be the one constant in an ever-changing world. Shakespeare, in his Sonnet 116, wrote on the virtue of constancy, saying that "Love is not love which alters when it alteration finds."

We ought not put people on pedestals, as if they should never fall or crack. We often do not live up to our own expectations, so we should not be surprised when others disappoint us. When people do not act as perfectly as we would like, we should still love them, and even more so, since in times of weakness they need our love all the more. "You can get more with honey (compassion) than you can with vinegar (judgment)." The greater the need, the more we should extend God's mercy to others.

Because love is such a personal thing, we have to be careful how we "fall into love." If we "fall in love," and that magnetic attraction which draws us together does not deepen into true love for the person, we can just as easily "fall out of love."

We grow to love each other through the seasons and years lived together. The more we learn about another, the more there is to love. When we look closely at a diamond, we are taken with its multi-faceted beauty, which reflects dazzling colors when held in the light. When we appreciate what the other person is all about, we seek to only see the good. The good beheld in the other should inspire us to express our love for that person in meaningful ways. Knowing that "beauty is in the eye of the beholder," we need to look at our spouse through the eyes of love, not holding back but telling our beloved that "this beholder is *enchanted*."

What Your Spouse Needs Most

What pleases the beloved most is to have the lover there at all times, or as much as possible, and to be paid attention to—even to be made the center of attention, as if she or he was the only person on earth at that moment. Can we give our spouses what they need most and like best, putting them before anyone or anything else? A man doesn't always have to give his wife money to make her happy (although she could use a little spending money). What she would rather have is a *"Baby, I love you!"* And then if you gave her some of her favorite flowers, a stuffed animal, or special snack, she wouldn't mind a bit! What she is looking for is an indication that her man has not forgotten her, but thinks about her often and lets her know it in ways she can't mistake.

Sometimes we feel like a sponge from which all the moisture has been drained. We may feel like we haven't much extra to give. We need the Lord to refresh and invigorate us so that we can show each other how much we care. God has shown us how much He loves us by giving us someone with the capacity to understand us better than anyone else, and someone who wants to share deeply in our thoughts and concerns. So, instead of saying with impatience, "Where's the food?" or, "Haven't you cooked yet?" we could say sweetly, "I missed you," or "Where's my kiss?" A few kind words or a compliment goes a long way with a person. Let's shower the people we love with our love, showing them how we are truly glad they are part of our lives. Throwing bouquets of affection is always welcome.

Let The Light In

And ye shall know the truth and the truth shall make you free (John 8:32). The truth is, we need to learn to give as well as receive! So now that we have received freely, we have the opportunity to freely give (Matthew 10:8). And who deserves to receive your love more than the one who has forsaken all others to be with you? Do we pause enough to consider that our spouse has set aside the possibilities that life might have offered on another path, had we not come into our spouse's life? You have both decided to throw in your lot with each other, to make a life together, one of your own making. So why not make it definitely worth each other's while? Show her that her decision to love you was the best decision she ever made, that she was the best choice you have ever chosen, and that the time you spend together is the best time of your lives.

And the Lord said, Let there be light: and there was light (Genesis 1:3).

Intimacy Is For All Times

We ought to feel free to express the warmth of emotion we have deep down for our beloved by reaching out and touching our spouse affectionately, giving a loving caress. Intimacy should be continual, warmly expressed with touch and encouraging words, not only for the purposes of having sex. Our union is to be more than just physical. If the only time we express our love for each other is in bed, there is no guarantee that our marriage will last. Love enkindled between human spirits, grown in the Holy Spirit, is what causes our love for each other to mature and endure. Maintaining intimacy does not consist only in physical touch either, but in a lifetime of tenderness expressed, the total amount of time lovingly shared. Our focus should be that of making our love last forever, by filling up our human love with the love in our spirit. Spiritual intimacy—a sense of oneness in our love for God—contributes to our human love. With this thought in mind, someone has coined the phrase, "holy passion!"

The phrase "The two will become one flesh" (I Corinthians 6:16), means much more than the physical unity of the two; it represents the spiritual union or marriage of souls. But as we are *embodied* spirits, touch is very important in maintaining that personal intimacy so indispensable in marriage. So too is the gentleness with which we treat each other.

God Loves Us "In Spite Of"

Christ looks at his bride with affection, for she is His—a *joy* no one can take from Him (John 16:22). God gave Himself as a ransom for her—that is how much she is worth to Him. He willingly emptied Himself even to the last drop of His blood shed on the cross; we are to love each other selflessly with His grace.

Christ didn't love us because we first loved him; He first loved us and made us capable of receiving, and responding to His love. He loved us *in spite of* our unlovable traits, so that we would do likewise:

> *Beloved, let us love one another: for love is of God; and everyone that loveth is born of God, and knoweth God. He that loveth not knoweth not God; for God is love. In this was manifested the love of God toward us, because that God sent his only begotten Son into the world, that we might live through him. Herein is love, not that we loved God, but that he loved us, and sent his Son to be the propitiation for our sins. Beloved, if God so loved us, we ought also to love one another. . . . If we love one*

another, God dwelleth in us, and his love is perfected in us. *Hereby know we that we dwell in him, and he in us, because he hath given us of his Spirit. And we have seen and do testify that the Father sent the Son* to be *the Saviour of the world* (I John 4:7-14, emphasis added).

Though He might not care for some of the things we do, God is incapable of hating people; He simply loves. We need to be more like Him and should pray earnestly for the grace daily. We just don't know how much we need Him! We must ask Him to increase our ability to love so that our lives will testify that we have received Jesus' message.

Love One Another

If we approach each other daily with divine love, when we are in the midst of the congregation, that pure love will be seen by everyone to the glory of God. In John 15:12, Jesus says *"This is my commandment, that ye love one another, as I have loved you."* He didn't say, "I want you to love based on how you feel," but "as I have loved you." The most hidden secrets of our lives have already been forgiven; we need to take in that forgiveness and extend it to others.

Greater love hath no man than this, that a man lay down his life for his friends. Ye are my friends, if ye do whatsoever I command you. Henceforth I call you not servants; for the servant knoweth not what his lord doeth; but I have called you friends; for all things that I have heard of my father I have made known unto you. Ye have not chosen me, but I have chosen you, and ordained you, that ye should go and bring forth fruit, and that your fruit should remain; that whatsoever ye shall ask of the Father in my name, he may give it you (John 15:13-17).

So, if we would love people with constancy, we would be denied nothing we ask of God. If we really want to be blessed, we must stop hating people. No matter what they have done to us, we must love them "in spite of" and we'll be amazed at what the Lord will do in our lives! Divine love surpasses our understanding and brings many graces upon us and our families. If everyone in our families and ministry expressed genuine, divine love for each other, we would not be able to imagine how powerful a witness would be given to our world!

Can't Live With You; Can't Shoot You

We should change *now,* so that we do not strain our relationships with people and do more harm than good. Instead of feeling safe enough with our loved ones so that we show them the nastiness we are capable of, we can show them how much we love them. It's much more enjoyable being around someone who concentrates only on giving, so let's focus on ourselves becoming a joy to be around.

But we need to look beyond people's misdeeds and lack of character in our eyes. Each of us needs to say to those who have offended us, "Yes, you might have done me wrong, but that's in the past—let's move on in the love of Christ!" When we make the transition from only loving those who have treated us well, we will have moved into the beginnings of divine love and what is called "repairing the breach":

> *Moreover the light of the moon shall be as the light of the sun, and the light of the sun shall be sevenfold, as the light of seven days, in the day that the Lord bindeth up the breach of his people, and healeth the stroke of their wound* (Isaiah 30:26).

Look Beyond

I used to say, "My spirit connects with your spirit." But if my spirit only connected with certain spirits, something is missing. We are supposed to be "all things for all men" (I Corinthians 10:33)—not limiting our association with people to whom we deem worthy, and not seeking to profit from the company of others as much as to invite them to draw a little closer to God. We have to connect with everyone. Jesus even loved Judas, of whom He said, *"Have not I chosen you twelve, and one of you is a devil"* (John 6:70).

We have to do everything we can to get others into the kingdom of God, even if our self-love is ruffled quite a bit. But what if someone doesn't like me, and that person is evil—how can I be connected at all with a person like that? We are commanded to love; when we truly love, we do not care what the other person does. Even if they do not respond to our love outwardly, or reject it, our job is to continue loving. We cannot force anyone to love us, but we can love them anyway. When we bless someone who has hurt us, we're building coals of fire—an altar and a memorial to the love of God—right there. That's what God wants—our hearts to be changed—and He'll work on the others.

Our example can be part of God's work in others. We are His Body in the world: His hands and feet to spread His love, and His eyes to look with compassion on this world. Since we demonstrate what is inside us by our words, deeds, and even "body language," let us give off the message of love and acceptance of the human person with all of its frailty because that is what Jesus did. For example, we need to love our pastor and support him, even if he doesn't say or do what we think he should *every time*.

Love That Unites and Endures

In John 21:15-19, Jesus was speaking of a supernatural level of love when He said to Peter, "Do you love me more than these?" Jesus wanted Peter to love God and his brethren on a divine level (*agape*), not just on a brotherly level. It would be Peter's responsibility to strengthen his brothers and keep them together under his leadership, once he himself had recovered (Luke 22:32). In humility, he was to serve his brothers just as Jesus—though the Master—was the servant of all. Peter was the one the Lord had chosen to guard the flock in the place of the Shepherd, so he had to have the heart of the Shepherd.

In like manner, God wants our love for our spouse to surpass merely brotherly love (*filio*) and sensual love (*eros*), reaching forth for the divine love that puts the beloved's needs before our own, to love the other as we love ourselves.

The Perspective of a Pastor's Wife

If we really want to improve the quality of our love, we can ask someone we love how our love is coming across. Do others feel our love? Are there areas our love can improve? Is there anything that we are doing that is causing a stumbling block to another's faith? Do we want others to do as we say but not as we do? Clearly, there is always room to improve, and one of the best ways is to find out how our spouses are feeling towards us, and if there is something more we can do for them that we are not already doing. I asked my wife Carol to offer her views on how we are to love in the spirit, and her testimony follows:

Webster's Dictionary describes the word *divine* as having the nature of a deity (a God-like form), inspired by, or devoted to a deity, and as being perfect. This supernatural love is what God expects us to have for each other as human beings, whether married or single. In I Corinthians 13, we hear about the unconditional love needed to acquire our rightful status here on earth as well as in heaven. Divine love can only be expressed from a person with a divinely inspired state of mind.

Both men and women are created by God, but they each have different expectations of love. In single-parent families, women are faced with the dual responsibility as mother and father figure. In more and more homes today, she is the only breadwinner of the immediate and extended family. She is the one who deals with emotional issues and helps fight spiritual or inward battles, and she encourages those struggling with low self-esteem, unreasonable treatment on the job, and lack of attaining educational goals. In addition, as part of her daily routine, this mother may suffer the utter frustration that can only be brought about by ungrateful and demanding children, without the consolation of even a monthly compliment from her spouse. With such a job description, how many would apply?

God requires everyone to love, and yet it seems that even a married woman has to wear more than one hat. Listen to what she is called to take on, and consider whether just anyone can do what she does—or even would want to—if given the choice.

> *Who can find a virtuous woman? for her price is far above rubies. The heart of her husband doth safely trust in her, so that he shall have no need of spoil. She will do him good and not evil all the days of her life. She seeketh wool and flax, and worketh willingly with her hands. She is like the merchants' ships; she bringeth her food from afar. She riseth also while it is yet night, and giveth meat to her household . . . with the fruit of her hands she planteth a vineyard. She girdeth her loins with strength, and strengtheneth her arms. She perceiveth that her merchandise is good; her candle goeth not out by night. . . . She stretcheth out her hand to the poor; yea, she reacheth forth her hands to the needy* (Proverbs 31:10-18,20).

The wife is to be the heart of refuge for her husband, strengthening herself for tackling all family issues, giving always to the needy in her household and outside it. She is to be an offering for the Lord, sparing herself little:

> *She is not afraid of the snow for her household; for all her household are clothed with scarlet. . . . Her husband is known in the gates, when he sitteth among the elders of the land. . . . Strength and honour are her clothing; and she shall rejoice in time to come. She openeth her mouth with wisdom; and in her tongue is the law of kindness. She looketh well to the ways of her household, and eateth not the bread of idleness* (Proverbs 31:21,23,25-27).

She is to speak with wisdom in love, care for her family in her husband's absence (which, according to v.23, appears to be quite often), and strength (virtue) and honor (holiness) are to clothe her. Much is expected of the woman of the household; may it please God to grant her all the grace she needs to fulfill her calling. In return, it is a blessing when *"Her children arise up, and call her blessed; her husband also, and he praiseth her"* (Proverbs 31:28).

But Jesus praises the spiritual receptivity of a woman over and above anything she does. In Luke 10:38-42, we see Martha literally about to lose her mind because of her sister's concern to sit and listen to Jesus, while the house needed to be redecorated for their special guest. In the end, Jesus actually complimented the one who listened to Him (Mary), instead of the sister who frenzied herself to insure a tasty meal, a clean house, and the hospitality to make sure everyone was taken care of. Her task is often thankless, and her effort goes seemingly unnoticed many times. Though not always receiving a proper return for all she does, God teaches her to be serene and to freely love. The majority of her time is spent doing, and precious few opportunities arise for quiet reflection. So we women want to be like Mary—collected, prayerful and peaceful—as we are doing like Martha, though we may find ourselves unequal to the task.

With prayer, women like Martha gain the heart of Jesus to love His people unconditionally. In fact, without bitterness, they attain the attributes of divine love (the fruit of the Spirit) when they can (almost) instantly forgive their spouse for not remembering a son's football game, a daughter's ballet recital, her own birthday, or at worst, a first wedding anniversary.

In today's busy world where the Church, community, workplace and economy are constantly changing, divine love needs to be renewed on a daily basis. Determination, or perseverance, is another need that we have in order to gain and show divine love. In Luke 8:43-48, a special woman had an issue of blood for 12 years and spent all her money on seeking a cure from physicians. This determined woman made her way through a multitude of possibly thousands to touch the Master in faith, believing He could solve her problem. Women have to be determined to handle everyday issues with love, which is the only answer to otherwise undesirable or impossible circumstances. Whether facing loneliness as widows or divorcées, confusion or disturbances as young, immature women facing heavy work loads and high expectations, we still have to ask for God's guidance and employ divine love to get us through and help us triumph in our lifetime.

Love can be implemented in every area of life. I certainly have experienced many forms of divine love as a child, teenager, and now a married woman of 13 years. As a child, I was privileged to not receive a single whipping from my parents. This mercy was possibly due to the fact that I was the only girl among several children. Or else it was divine love which spared me, because in those days everyone got punished or a beating for the simplest error.

Another facet of perfect love was demonstrated to me as a teenager, when my mother risked losing her job to bring me a tomato for my cooking class at school, which I needed to decorate the corner of a dish filled with macaroni and cheese. I only called her once, and she brought it right away. Love is often shown in the little things rather than in what others would consider "big" favors. To me, bringing that tomato was as big as it gets. Showing loving attention by picking up on our children's needs and responding to them speaks more loudly than anything else we could do for them. Care like that says to a child—and even a spouse—that you know and understand me better than anyone. They can really *feel* your love. To love as Jesus, above all we must want to seek to understand the needs of those God gives us a relationship with. We must make them feel special, just as my mother did for me.

As a married woman, it takes love, respect, communication, and unceasing love to maintain my marriage as a woman, a wife—and most of all—a pastor's wife. In Genesis 2:23-24, the Word declares,

> *This is now bone of my bones and flesh of my flesh; she shall be called "woman" for she was taken out of a man...*

For this reason a man will leave his father and mother and be united to his wife, and they will become one flesh.

A woman generally has to realize that, once she enters the vocation of matrimony, her entire lifestyle as a single woman changes, and a heart of divine love must be placed in her to enable her to support and help her spouse and to understand his ways.

Love is not usually measured by quantity, but rather by quality and sincerity of heart, even if it's a small gesture. Most women would agree that they would like to receive one gift of candy, a pair of pantyhose, or even a rose petal on a monthly basis, rather than receive no gift or verbal praise for an entire year. Both spouses like to be remembered and appreciated for who they are and what they bring into their marriage covenant. In the same way, wives should thank their husbands for the sacrifices they make in providing for their household and for a job well done.

I felt my husband's divine love for me on a particular occasion in January, 1985 (I remembered when it happened). Henry, my fiancé at the time, called me from the subway corner of Nostrand and Sterling Street in Brooklyn, New York, to tell me he had something special for me. In a few minutes, he was at my door with a wide grin on his face and one hand behind his back. Of course, I was somewhat startled, knowing he only had his token money to take the train. He told me to put out one hand and close my eyes. When I opened my eyes, I beheld a palm-sized bag of "Mama's fries" from my favorite place, "Mama's Kitchen," located by the subway. I was more than appreciative because I knew he bought it with all the money he had because it was my favorite snack. If that is not an expression of divine love, I do not know what is.

In this manner of giving what matters most—our love for each other—I've learned to appreciate love in the simplest way, even if it means just letting a little child with sticky fingers give me a bear hug while I'm dressed for Sunday services! Henry's surprise was a very humble yet loving example of the beginning of our relationship. In spite of our hectic schedules of counseling and praying with people, and planning and implementing growth in the ministry God has called us to, we still strive to show our tender love for each other, especially on the twentieth of each month—the day of our anniversary.

From God's viewpoint on divine love, a woman needs to receive love, attention, respect, care and reassurance. Almost automatically, most women will respond to her man's love by showing approval and appreciation to him for fulfilling her needs and for caring about her as a person in the most personal ways imaginable. In Ephesians 5:22-23, Paul wrote about the need that spouses had to fulfill in their marriage: to develop, maintain, and keep ever new a spousal, almost-perfect, divine love for each other. God's command to man is to love his wife as much as he loves himself; likewise, the bride should reverence her own husband. Women are also encouraged to show love and compassion to those women who have been molested, raped, physically or emotionally abused, and seem to have an irreversibly low self-esteem.

If more spouses and other true woman believers would share this divine love and heartfelt concern, our world would be a kinder place for both men and women to love each other in a surpassing, unconditional manner. Infinite love can be expressed in very human, endearing ways. Jesus showed us that touch and a kind way of speaking to a loved one can have supernatural power, as exemplified in Jesus raising Jairus' 12 year old daughter from the dead by gently taking her hand and bidding her to arise. She responded by getting up and walking, and Jesus instructed that she be given something to eat (Mark 5:38-43). Jesus thinks of everything, and cares for us most personally. This limitless Godlike love is what we are to give freely to those God puts before us, and those with whom we must lovingly dwell each day.

Chapter Three
Forgiveness Transforms

For if ye love them which love you . . . and . . . do good to them, what thank have ye? . . . Be ye therefore merciful, as your Father also is merciful. . . . Give, and it shall be given unto you; good measure, pressed down, and shaken together, and running over, shall men give into your bosom. For with the same measure that ye mete withal it shall be measured to you again . . . Can the blind lead the blind? shall they not both fall into the ditch? The disciple is not above his master: but every one that is perfect shall be as his master (Luke 6:32-33,36,38-40).

The Way It Is Now

No matter how much we try to love people from the heart, we find our human love often limited by forgiving only initially and yet remembering and holding onto the pain in our heart. After living a while, we accumulate a number of hurts or emotional wounds which render us unable to love freely without fear of rejection. We become less likely to disclose who we really are. Thus, if we do open up and express our love, we do so only when we feel safe—when the other person is judged trustworthy of not hurting your feelings. We go to those who we know will give us the response we want, and tend to avoid those who do not.

But even with those we like, we are cheerful and easy-going with them when they are good to us, but if they stumble over our weak areas or sore spots, we are going to let them know about it, or at least hold it against them. We will likely try to get them back not only for the wounds they have caused us but all the others we have suffered as well. In this way we build impenetrable barriers that we cannot remove by ourselves, and tend to seek non-threatening company and conversations. God has to open up our hearts and heal them so that He can pour in His healing love, which overcomes all resistances and elevates our love beyond human limitations. *The power of forgiveness is unlimited.* Merciful, all-forgiving love is what Jesus displayed on the cross—Him whose very heart was pierced by a lance. We must admit we do not want to suffer the same fate, and yet that is what He asks of us, if we would be like Him and be truly free.

How Our Love Can Become

We must not love based on the condition of our heart, giving only what we in our littleness think we can afford to give. We must love according to the condition of His sacred heart which burns with a consuming yet never exhausted love for us. He loves us with a veritable furnace of charity; what return of our love shall we make in response? We cannot outdo God in generosity, but we do want to give our best with His help.

See if He will not turn our love into the compassionate love of His divine heart. Like the woman with the hemorrhage in the Gospel, who touched the fringe of His garment, we too can feel an increase, influx, and insurge of the power of love in our lives directly from the fountain of His inexhaustible strength. Because of our faith in His power, we will be "made whole" (Matthew 9:20-22). We can drink from the wellspring that never runs dry nor ceases to satisfy us (John 4:14). Full of His love, we will be enabled to worship the Father in spirit and in truth (John 4:23). Our love will be elevated as with Jesus on the cross, drawing all men unto Him (John 12:32).

Bitterness Holds Us Back

But before we reach for the divine, we must deal with what humanly hinders us. Unforgiveness will cause three things to occur in our lives. The first effect of unforgiveness is bitterness. When you truly forgive someone, you have actually allowed yourself to overlook what they have done; you have released them from your heart. Forgiveness is saying, "I pardon you, and I erase your debt." In sharp contrast, unforgiveness says, "I will not forgive you until the day I die." Without grace, we hold onto the pain our whole lives and might not get the chance to make peace before we die. How good it is to be reconciled before time gets away from us! How sad it is for us to carry for many years burdens of the unhappy things people have done to us. We make a mistake if we say, "I forgive you, but I'll never forget it."

A Toll on the Body

Not only does our soul remain less than beautiful due to our refusal to love beyond the pain and come up higher to embrace divine love, but our physical condition may also suffer because of it. Beyond not eating, sleeping, or taking care of ourselves as we would if something was not bothering us, our hidden pain may eventually manifest itself on our bodies in the form of ulcers, cancerous tumors, arthritis, heart problems, and breathing difficulties. We literally "rot our own guts," building up fluids or acids that are harmful to our health and cause it to break down. Cancer cells, for example, are cells "gone crazy," which have turned malignant and reproduce out of control. The stress of living with the pain of a broken or lost close personal relationship, especially that of a parent or spouse surely can contribute to our bodies not functioning as they should. Our emotions are powerful agents which cause physical reactions in the body, which is like crying on the inside. We need God to heal us, and forgiveness begins that process.

Forgive and Be Free

Though we may not be aware of it, we are in pain on the inside and need the Divine Physician to make us whole. Jesus came to pay the price for all our sins—past, present and future. He chooses not to remember them, but prefers to see what we will become in His love. He does not ever come up to you and remind you of your past. If we are doing that to others, we are not living a victorious life, which is based on overcoming and helping others to overcome. Unforgiveness is a stumbling block that reduces us to crawling when we could soar like an eagle. We have to forgive as we have been forgiven by God, and as we'd *like* to be forgiven by our brothers and sisters.

The Lord's Prayer asks God to forgive us as we have forgiven our neighbors. We had better forgive others with the love of God, who forgets offenses. How can we ask God to forgive us the things that we have not forgiven our neighbor of? (see Matthew 18:27-35). How can we say we love God and not love the brother or sister sitting next to us. We cannot sit down at the wedding banquet, the table of the Lord, when we have not first "cleared the air" with our brethren. We need to release our pain so that others might be free, including ourselves.

One cause for bitterness is unforgiveness toward our parents. They may have done us wrong or simply were not there for us. We wanted so much to feel their love but came away feeling disappointed because they were not able to express it as much as we needed it, or as often as we would have liked. If they are still a part of our lives, we have to try to love them for how they *do* try to love us, and let every other concern go. "Honor thy father and mother" still applies, even when it *is* difficult.

Should I Stay or Should I Go?

Another critical area needing attention is that of bitter relationships between couples. Though the faithfulness and perpetual love of God for His Church is what we are called to follow as His people, we do recognize that human weakness is a factor in the choices we have made, for whatever reason. God never intended for some unfortunate unions to come about. One woman married a man because he wanted to marry her, and she couldn't find the strength within herself to say, "No, this isn't right for me." She told her mother of her uncomfortableness the night before the wedding, and wished her father would come and take her away from what she feared would be a terrible mistake. Her concern was dismissed as "cold feet," and she was encouraged to go ahead with it. They married, but because they were not truly right for each other, or "unequally yoked," they ended up getting divorced. We find often ourselves in situations that are hard to get ourselves out, short of an act of God.

Love Conquers All

When one of the two, or both, decide not to love the other forever, unhappiness results. If God can be brought into the situation, there is hope for saving the relationship. God does commend our striving after heroic, sacrificial love which knows no limitation; we pray for His grace that we might attain it. With our patient perseverance, God can grow in us and our spouse the sort of mature love that He wants for all of us. By humble submission and reverence for each other out of love for Christ, many have overcome intolerable situations.

I have seen God restore the love of a wife for her husband after he was unfaithful to her. This husband had lived apart from her for some time, and God caused him to want to be reconciled, and to love his wife. He told her that God had motivated him to come back into her life. As you would expect, she wanted nothing to do with the man, couldn't stand the sight of him. After a few good short meetings with him, God told her He wanted her to let her husband live in her house once again. She submitted—not without serious reservations—provided he not come near her. This delicate living arrangement continued for some time, as God worked on both of their hearts, as He was doing all along. Their love was restored miraculously. Only God could do that.

God knows what will make you most happy in life (Himself) and has in mind the person that can best bring you to Him and fill your heart with His love. If we seek His perfect will, He will reveal that person to us, and we may be surprised at who it is.

The Lord Is Our Source

In the way of fellowship, we look for people who will pay attention to us, value what we deem important and validate us for who we are and what we are capable of becoming with the help of Almighty God. We seek a spouse who will look beyond our exterior to the real person inside, and love us. Such a perception is indeed quite rare; it requires the ability of the other to respond to us and give us the love we need. People without such graces cannot give us what we are looking for, because they haven't first received them in order to give. We can't treat a person like a store, expecting them to have what we want. Sometimes, they haven't any artichokes.

A woman went into a store looking for artichokes, but found none, no matter whom she asked. She was insistent on receiving what she wanted, but finally left unhappy. Later, someone told her that he knew that a store down the street had some. Unhappiness can result from looking in the wrong places for what we need.

In general, people cannot give us what they do not have, be it understanding, love, or a certain reaction we are looking for. We have to "take it from where we can get it," and accept and love others regardless. Much frustration, anger, bitterness and emptiness can be averted by going to the source—Jesus—and the special vessels He provides. When we experience freedom from self-imposed burdens, peace, understanding, mercy, reconciliation, and love can then fill our hearts. Our release is the key to our helping others to change. When we stop making demands that our expectations be met, others may change how they relate to us.

Oddly enough, the opposite of what we expect to happen (our surrender, rather than theirs) brings about more of what we would like to happen. With regard to our spouse, we have to be careful not to expect something they can't give. We have to remember that only in God is our soul at complete rest (see Psalms 62 and 63). Fellowship with other Christians may help fill in the gap, but we are to look to the Lord as our ultimate source of fulfillment and satisfaction.

An Absence of the Fruit

Besides bitterness, unforgiveness comes from an ignorance of the Word of God, and therefore an absence of the fruit of the Spirit:

But the fruit of the Spirit is love, joy, peace, longsuffering, gentleness, goodness, faith, meekness, temperance: against such there is no law. And they that are Christ's have crucified the flesh with the affections and lusts. If we live in the Spirit, let us also walk in the Spirit. Let us not be desirous of vain glory, provoking one another, envying one another (Galatians 5:22-26).

If we do not forgive, we will be less inclined to love, express joy, have peace, be patient, gentle and good. We will have difficulty believing others and therefore tend toward cynicism. It will be hard to be meek, we will prefer rather to attack in order to defend ourselves. We will more easily lose our self-control in testy situations and even in small annoyances.

For in the spirit, we learn to resist our natural tendencies and take on the divine likeness of Christ. He actually removed the power of sin over our lives by His cross; it is up to us to appropriate or bring internally the gifts He has given us to triumph over the ways of our flesh which seem right to us but only bring us death. To choose the way that leads to life, we are not to provoke one another, regardless of who is right; rather we are to win others over by our example. If we forgive, we will not walk in ignorance of the ways of the God who wants to give us every *good* thing.

Walking in the Flesh

The third thing unforgiveness does is make us walk in ignorant, fleshly desires. Unforgiveness makes us want to hurt someone—spouse, church member, or stranger. An acclaimed ABC network television special, called "Road Rage," documented how an ordained minister got out of his car, argued with another traveller, and shot the man with his crossbow. He is now serving a lifetime prison sentence. Another irate driver, after bumping cars in an attempt to "be first," began shooting at what he thought was his competitor, filling his driver-side door with bullets, killing the man's 21-year-old girlfriend instead. The only thing he thought he should have done differently was go to the hospital; he didn't think he could act differently under the circumstances. Too often we feel that we have no choice, and live *under* the circumstances, reacting to life's circumstances in the flesh. Our hearts need to be encouraged, redeemed, and healed so that we can live in the Spirit.

We *Do* Have a Choice

How can we deal with unforgiveness? First we are to look at God. Regardless of what we did, He gave totally of Himself, sparing nothing—not even His Son. He gave everything so that we could have everything—eternal life in His divine love. We need to give God that part of ourselves that stubbornly refuses to give and wants to preserve self for pride's sake. If you are selfish, you may find it harder to forgive, and unforgiveness will take its place in you, a place that was meant to be filled with love. We can allow no part of us not to be filled with love; we must allow God entrance to every part of our being if we are to be all His.

> *As many as I love, I rebuke and chasten; be zealous, therefore, and repent. Behold I stand at the door and knock; if any man hear my voice, and open the door, I will come in to him, and will sup with him, and he with me* (Revelation 3:19-20).

When God gives you divine love, correction will not offend you. Some folks run from a church when they have been corrected. But the way we grow is to listen and obey, even when it hurts to do so. If we won't let anyone talk to us to help us when we are in need, we may open ourselves to danger. With no input from others, we may fall into blindness and our conscience may be dulled unknowingly. Unforgiveness then may come and engulf us because we are not willing to be corrected. We need endurance and longsuffering (patience). We can't quit our job over any little thing; if we don't forgive, how can God use us? We are not going to find a perfect situation to rest ourselves in; each place will have its trials, ups and downs. Despite whatever advantages one opportunity offers, we may have to sacrifice in other ways not immediately detectable at first glance.

People are people; they are imperfect. They will misunderstand you, talk about you, and mistreat you; this we can expect. We have faults, too, and they have to deal with ours.

Behold, I send you forth as sheep in the midst of wolves. Be ye, therefore, wise as serpents and harmless as doves (Matthew 10:16).

Release yourself from your bonds of bitterness by acts of kindness; at the same time, be wise and do not leave yourself overly vulnerable so that they can hurt you again. Do not speak well-meaning words that will cause them to react against you; do not cast your pearls among the swine who will trample them and then turn on you (Matthew 7:6). Let the Lord's presence in you be your witness; do what He wants you to do and speak only what He would have you, and no more.

We can even get creative in our approach to handling people who hurt us. We can invite them to dinner at our home, take them to a concert and pay for their tickets, give them a thoughtful present on their birthday and tell them something about them that inspires you, give them some food if you think they would like it and could use it, thank them for the way that they support what you are doing, thank them for putting up with your work performance if you've been sick, and so on. By acting in this winning way, they will have nothing to accuse you of and will be compelled to think differently about you. One thing is for sure, they won't know what to do with you now, but may want to imitate you some time in the future. Forgiveness in the Spirit is the way to transform not only your own life, but those around you!

Where Divine Love Takes Up

Therefore if any man be in Christ, he is a new creature: old things are passed away; behold, all things are become new (II Corinthians 5:17).

By praying the prayer of confession—confessing the *Lordship* of Jesus in our lives—our hearts experience a transformation of love. When we accept the boundless love of Jesus Christ in our heart, the quality and quantity of our love increases by leaps and bounds. The only limit to His love in us is how much we will allow Him to pour out. As we grow in His love, He will increase our capacity to give, making it more like His. The function of the human heart is elevated to that of God's own heart. Each day as we read the Word of God, we find that the old man is replaced by the new man. When the heart is changed, we have a renewed mind. Accepting Jesus Christ in our life means that we no longer live in the flesh but in the Spirit. A renewed mind does the perfect will of God.

For example, when we see faults in people, the first thing we do is *criticize* them. But if we do the will of God, we will restore them with love: *"If any man be overtaken in a fault, ye which are spiritual restore such a one in the spirit of meekness"* (Galatians 6:1). We should love people the way God loves us and restore them in His way. They will know we are Christians by our love (John 13:35). Love is proof that we have the Spirit of God.

Human love does not operate in the will of God—it cannot because it operates by the flesh. The flesh cannot please God for it is selfish, concerned with no one else but itself. But God is not selfish: He went the extra mile to show us what divine love really is—He sent His Son to die for our sins. We cannot really love people without loving them through Jesus Christ; and for us to do this, we must have a transformed mind:

And be not conformed to this world: but be ye transformed by the renewing of your mind, that ye may prove what is that good and acceptable and perfect will of God (Romans 12:2).

A transformed mind will bring you into the will of God. The only things that are acceptable to God are the good things He had in His will for us. We either do it *His* way or *our* way; if we do things His way, we will be blessed without measure. One of the most merciful ways we are blessed by His love is the forgiveness of our sins. God's love is so great that He wants to cover our sins and clothe us with His righteousness:

And above all things have fervent charity among yourselves: for charity shall cover the multitude of sins (I Peter 4:8).

People tend to be revengeful when someone offends them; the norm is to fight back. But here we see God will cover and remove our sins—no matter how many they might be. He is always ready to love us through Jesus Christ. He does not dwell on our past and tell others about what we have done. Instead, He always sees the good in us and views us as we will be in heaven.

About seven years ago, Carol and I were youth pastors at a local church in south Florida. When we started in our new positions, things were going great until one day the pastor began listening to a group of people who disliked me. Because he believed what he had heard, the pastor decided to confront me publically—from the pulpit. It was said that I was plotting to take his church, so he went public and embarrassed me. He said some things that were hurtful and demeaning to my character.

At first, the flesh—which is human love—said to me that I should fight back, curse him and challenge him openly. But God's kind of love was able to rein me in and encourage me to love and forgive him, since he was acting on second-hand information that was not verified. It was extremely hard for me not to respond as I was treated. But the Word was in my heart, planted in my soul with the power to save me (James 1:21) so that I would not sin or even enter into temptation.

Thy word have I hid in my heart, that I might not sin against thee (Psalms 119:11).

If husbands would apply the Word of God in their marriage, we would find that our wives would love us in a more biblical way. If my marriage seems to fall on the more human side of love, I will only love my spouse for what she can do for me. That kind of love will last as long as people do what pleases us; but when they fail to please us, we tend to express our dissatisfaction. In I Peter 3:1, we find the way God wants us to love in marriage, to patiently win each other over to God's love:

Likewise, ye wives, be in subjection to your husbands; that, if any obey not the word, they also may without the word be won by the conversation of the wives.

Those wives who have a husband in need of redemption are to love him with the spirit of submission and win him to the Lord Jesus Christ.

Likewise, ye husbands, dwell with them according to knowledge, giving honor unto the wife (I Peter 3:7).

Husbands are to love their wives with the knowledge and wisdom of God, knowing that the thoughts of their wives are different from their own. We must try to understand them and not let our feelings get in the way. When our emotions interfere with our relationship, we cannot love as we ought. We must not get upset when we are tested in our relationship. The purpose of our trials is to give us a testimony. A common thing that men do when they feel pressured at home is to leave and try to find an alternative resting place. But when we have divine love in our hearts, we will dwell together—and stick it out—to the end.

The Marriage Vows

I will take this woman to be my wedded wife, to live together in the holy state of matrimony; I will love her, comfort her, honor her and keep her, in sickness and in health, and forsaking all others, keep yourself only to her so long as we both shall live.

When I married Carol, my commitment was to keep her forever—to dwell with her and never leave her, loving her as Jesus loves. In Hebrews 13:5, God said, *"I will never leave you, nor forsake you."* When we love the way God wishes us to love, we will not want to quit so easily. The more we read the Word, the more we will find that human love can be replaced when we have the love of Jesus in our lives. This healing transition will take place when we are renewed in our minds and put what we have learned into consistent action, even if we still fall short occasionally.

The greatest Bible story on divine love is found in Luke 15:11-20. Here we see a young man going to his father and asking for his inheritance. After receiving his portion, he went into a distant country and wasted his substance on riotous living.

Now his father could have gone to his elder son and complained bitterly about what his younger son did. It would have been easy for him to change the locks on the doors of his home and instruct his faithful son not to open the door to him should he decide to come back home. But according to verse 20, the father waited for him patiently, knowing he made a mistake and that he might need help in the future. He must have prayed that his son have his mind renewed, be reconciled and reunited with the family. He waited compassionately for his boy; and when he arrived safely home, he opened his heart to him. He forgave and forgot and so was he able to love him with God's love, which we know in our hearts is what we have wanted all our lives.

God gives us tremendous grace and the opportunities to let others feel from us the love of *the Father*. The Father forgets our wanderings from His love and loves us tenderly as His returning children—who in His heart never left. That love expresses what it means to live in the will of God.

Forgetting those things which are behind, and reaching forth unto those things which are before (Philippians 3:13).

The father fulfilled this scripture from Philippians: he forgave his son and renewed his relationship with him. He was not so concerned with what his son did as much as how he could have a better relationship with him in the present and future. We know that overlooking and going beyond what holds *us* back is difficult. Our feelings have been hurt, but the love of God is stronger—it cannot be offended.

> *Charity suffereth long,* and *is kind; charity envieth not; charity vaunteth not itself, is not puffed up, doth not behave itself unseemly, seeketh not her own, is not easily provoked, thinketh no evil* (I Corinthians 13:4-5).

This father's love waited a long time for his son to come home; he waited with limitless patience and He was kind to his son when he returned. How many times do we wait, only to vent our frustration at being made to suffer in uncertainty; we tend to express our brokenness rather than the love and concern we really do feel deep down. But this father was kind to his son—a feat worth repeating! He was not provoked by his son's request but gave him what he wanted. Our God likewise allows us to do what we want, and He forgives us for not asking Him what He wants for us. We cannot truly love and choose what is best for us until we experience the love that God has for us. When we can take in His love, we will want all that He has for us. We will have his heart in exchange for our own, and give His love freely to others and especially in a lasting way to our spouse.

Chapter Four
Leave It Behind

Forgive and Forget

Then came Peter to him, and said, Lord, how oft shall my brother sin against me, and I forgive him? till seven times? Jesus saith unto him, I say not unto thee, Until seven times: but, Until seventy times seven. Therefore is the kingdom of heaven likened unto a certain king, which would take account of his servants. And when he had begun to reckon, one was brought unto him which owed him ten thousand talents. . . . The servant therefore fell down and worshipped him, saying, Lord, have patience with me, and I will pay thee all. Then the lord of that servant was moved with compassion, and loosed him, and forgave him the debt (Matthew 18:21-24,26-27).

Why didn't the fortunate man—released from an enormous debt by his master—turn and forgive his brother who owed him little in comparison (Matthew 18:28-35)? We employ a double standard that says we are to be forgiven our large character flaws while holding others to account for their insignificant irritating habits. Our scales of measurement have to be tipped in our brother's favor.

In order to love with a complete, spiritual, self-sacrificing love, we have to set aside the records we have kept of others' offenses toward us. We can no longer "save stamps." Have we heard of relatives not visiting family in the hospital because this favor was not accorded to them when they were in need? We have been taught to treat others better than we do ourselves, but our tendency is to only return the treatment we have been given or even give less love back. We are sometimes like clams that need to be forced open, begrudging to give what little we have. God wants to heal us so we can share more with others, and in turn, receive more.

> *But this* I say, *he that soweth sparingly shall reap also sparingly; and he which soweth bountifully shall also reap bountifully. Every man according as he purposeth in his heart,* so let him give; *not grudgingly, or of necessity: for God loveth a cheerful giver* (II Corinthians 9:6-7).

We Need to Change *First*

How can people forget our sins if we keep committing them? We don't give people the chance to forget our faults. Some wives may say, "Pastor, you don't understand: I have forgotten it so many times, but it's just to much for me to bear—he's doing it over and over. I forgive him, and then he does it again. I'm tired of it—I'm frustrated—I'm fed up!" Repentance and conversion are required; the behavior must change. We have to be freed from what holds us back, and free others to do the same.

But first we need to tend to changing *ourselves,* before others will be changed. As couples we have to learn to look only to our spouse for personal fulfillment, and ultimately look to God for what we are still incapable of giving each other as human beings. We can pray for what we lack in ourselves and stop speaking of what we see as lacking in others. Our own lack of charity exceeds that which we convict others of; we have enough faults of our own to keep us busy (Matthew 7:3-5).

Easier Said Than Done

The Church must set the example. We have to walk the talk, instead of justifying our refusal to love. We talk about being able to live together in peace and even charity, and then we cooperate with the enemy whose intention is to destroy marriages because they are signs of God's love for us, his Church. Divorce in the Church is at an all-time high. We have to put aside the old ways of behaving that are not building up our families and the Body of Christ as a whole. We can't live in the past with our fleshly mode of operation. We have to listen to a message we don't want to hear—what does not please our flesh—if we are to grow. We can't afford to do things our own way in our own time. *We need to do what God wants us to do, how He wants us to do it, in His time!* We can't escape God; the Holy Spirit knows what no one else knows about us.

Don't Look Back

Why do we dig up the old man, when there's so much ahead in Christ? Let's do as Jesus said: *"Follow me, and let the dead bury their dead"* (Matthew 8:22). Living in the past will destroy you spiritually. Learning from the past is good, and the past should be used as a ladder of success; but you should never live in, dwell in, and feed on the past, because it will not fill your heart with the love you need.

And be not conformed to this world, but be ye transformed by the renewing of your mind (Romans 12:2).

Some Christians are living in the past because their minds are not renewed. Our minds have not been fully cleansed yet. In Psalm 23:5, David said, *"thou anointest my head with oil,"* because that is where the mind is, and it needs very much to be anointed in order to follow God, who is holy.

Wake the Sleeping Giant

We tend to think that the enemy dwells far from us, in the "dark continent" of Africa, or in Haiti. We seem to think that demons are readily identifiable as dark, ugly looking creatures acting crazy right in front of us—but that's how obvious they'd have to appear in order for us to recognize them! We are not accustomed to looking with our spiritual eyes.

We don't have to take the assault of the enemy as something against which we are helpless. Instead, get your mind renewed, and God will break the chains of the enemy on your life! The precious blood of Jesus is stronger than any other force on this earth or under it. How do you apply the Blood to your life? Carry on with spiritual warfare by praying, fasting, reading the Word, confessing your sins, receiving communion, and worshipping the Lord for who He is and the victory He is working out on your behalf! Immerse yourself in the Word so that you cease gossiping and ignore it when you hear it. The Word of God states in Philippians 4:8 that you should fill your mind with these things: whatever is honest, just, pure, lovely, of good report, virtuous, and praiseworthy. Holy things are the opposite of what demons want you to think and the last thing they want to hear spoken.

Be Anointed With Power

What the enemy wants us to think about and speak about is anything that keeps us out of God's holy presence. If he can't stop you from being a Christian, he will try to prevent you from being a holy one like Jesus. Just as he wanted to steer Jesus off the path that the Father had for him (Luke 4:1-13), he wants to do the same to you, so that you end up serving him.

When people live their lives close to God, there is power, and the enemy doesn't want God's power to be displayed at any cost. If you want to know what makes the enemy nervous, just look at what Jesus did after He withstood all of the enemy's temptations:

> *And Jesus returned in the* power of the Spirit *into Galilee: and there went out a fame of him through all the region round about. And he taught in their synagogues, being glorified of all. . .And when he had opened the book, he found the place where it was written, The Spirit of the Lord is upon me, because he hath* anointed *me to preach the gospel to the poor; he hath sent me to heal the brokenhearted, to preach* deliverance *to the*

captives, and recovering of sight to the blind, to set at liberty them that are bruised, to preach the acceptable year of the Lord (Luke 4:14-15,17-19, emphasis added).

Notice that Jesus was filled with the *power* of the Spirit; the people then received His words by that same Spirit who helps us to hear what God is speaking to us; and God was *glorified* among them. The Spirit *anointed* Him to perform a mighty work to the glory of the Father who sent Him. He would then bring about *deliverance* for the captives of every kind, reaching out and saving the lost. By his opening and closing the book, we see that He did everything with *authority*—having the first and last word on everything, as only God can—and telling the people that a most decisive moment in their salvation history was happening right in front of them (Luke 4:21).

Obey and Be Blessed

Blessings of faith that result in power poured out to save, to heal, and to glorify God are the fruits of obedience. Speaking only what God wants you to say has profound influence over what sort of ministry and witness you will have. Jesus did not falter in His loyalty to His Father and His way of doing things. Therefore, He would not turn stones into bread and thus break the fast that was preparing Him for battle (Luke 4:2-4). Breaking bread in a way that would tempt Him to sin would have also been a form of idolatry, betraying the one true God. Secondly, He would not speak words that would have placed the enemy in God's place of authority (Luke 4:5-8). And lastly, He would not do anything—like throwing Himself down from the pinnacle of the temple—that would attempt to force God's hand to do anything (Luke 4:9-12).

Walk in the Spirit

So, we must rightly avoid certain dangers that would cause the Spirit of God to depart from us. But the Holy Spirit must fill up the places in our hearts made by the departure of the former things. We must walk in the Spirit if we would be completely free. If we claim to love God and do not walk in His ways, then the last state we enter into will be worse than the first; if before we were troubled by one spirit, upon our clearing and cleaning up the place of our soul, the enemy will only be too pleased to bring seven spirits more deadly than the first (Matthew 12:45). We must be wise, and put into practice what we have learned in order for God to use us, which is what we want above all.

Stay Focused

But what do we do when those nagging memories of so many hurts and pains that we have caused others, and those that others have visited upon us, weigh heavily upon us? If we can make amends by treating others that much better today, giving of ourselves like never before, then God uses those memories for good— as long as we are acting not out of guilt, but out of love, the love that God wants us to continually shower on our brothers and sisters. But if the enemy is heaping condemnation upon you so as to discourage you, cause you to despair, and make you feel unworthy to ever serve God, then calmly dismiss those thoughts as so many flies (Beelzebub means "lord of the flies") that must not distract the believer from receiving nourishment and living as he would like. Forget the past, and stay focused.

Be Humble and Reach Forward

Your family history does not determine what you can accomplish by the grace of God. Because your family was poor does not mean that it will always be that way for you. I myself came from a household that slept in an aluminum room with an aluminum roof and walls with holes in them such that you could peer inside without difficulty. I lived under those conditions in Jamaica.

In Brooklyn, New York, at the time when I proposed to my wife Carol, I was making $68 a week. How many women would take someone up on such an offer? Most women would say, "Get behind me, satan!"

We would prefer to make 68 dollars per *hour,* never mind per week. I had to work as a messenger boy, walking 15 blocks in the snow wearing a shoe with a big hole in it (it was my only pair). When I got home, I would put my feet next to the heater just to warm them up. Anyone who has lived up north knows that the worst thing you can do when you're cold is put yourself up against the heater: it's like sticking yourself with thousands of pins and needles. I've been there, and it was not a pleasant experience.

When my wife and I were married, we moved down to Florida without money, and with no relatives or friends that could help us out financially. On the way to Florida we took a pound of beef pot-roast that Carol's mom cooked; we called it "the miracle beef," because with each day I cut a piece for dinner, the bigger that beef got!

As time went by, we found eviction notices on our door that read, "In three days, you'd better get out." We were saved, went to church, and spoke in tongues—and this is how we were treated? But I didn't look back where I came from, because I knew where I was going. I never despised my upbringing, for I was taught by my parents not to be proud of circumstances or possessions. *Humility will take you far.* The Bible speaks of the blessings that come with humbling ourselves in the sight of God: He guides the humble in what is right (Psalms 25:9); the Lord sustains the humble (Psalms 147:6); and He crowns the humble with salvation (Psalms 149:4).

We started by going to a church in Miami. There were days I had to mix and match clothes to make it look like I had enough suits. But we worked together and stuck it out *together*. At that point our pasts didn't matter: all we had was the present, and we looked to the Lord to provide for our future. We said, "You know, Lord, this is what we would like to do. We're going to be focused now: we know where You want to take us. And we started "doing" because we felt led to pursue our goal and follow our dream.

While we were trying so hard to be faithful to what God had called us, the enemy sent people to distract us and have us turn back from what God had for us—just as the enemy came against Jesus in the desert—when we were weak and at our lowest. They said to us, "You're not going to come out as anything. You're history!" and so on. They were really attacking Him who sent us, for I knew we could do nothing of ourselves.

Armed only with His charity and peace, God blessed us mightily, and we owe everything to Him. When you've got that divine love in your heart and know that God loves you in spite of yourself, you cannot ultimately be defeated. God looks at us through the blood of Jesus—He sees us as redeemed—the miracle God destined us to be. Regardless of what we were, He is making us pure as He is pure:

> *Behold, what manner of love the Father hath bestowed upon us, that we should be called the sons of God . . . Beloved, now are we the sons of God, and it doth not yet appear what we shall be: but we know that, when he shall appear, we shall be like him; for we shall see him as he is. And every man that hath this hope in him purifieth himself, even as he is pure* (I John 3:1-3).

Even if you've tried many things and failed, and found it impossible to perfect yourself, look to Him who makes us one, who gives us strength and binds every broken heart, and is giving us His heart to love His people.

Chapter Five
Onward and Upward
He Knows What He Is About

God does not want us to dwell on the past any more; He does not want you to measure everything based on how you had it before or even as it stands now. We must not be self-satisfied nor dissatisfied with our conditions, but be assured that we are where He wants us. What He has given us is enough to sustain us, otherwise He would change it. God wants to act so as to press toward the future, to learn and grow where we are right now so that we will be prepared to take on what He has for us later. Nothing we are experiencing is wasted or useless, but serves a purpose we may not be aware of at this time.

Expect Opposition

Every one of us has a future and a purpose specifically mapped out for us by Christ, should we choose His plan for us. Never think to yourself that the present situation is hopeless and that your anguish is inescapable. The enemy wants you to think you're never going to make it, so that you may as well quit. But you can make it if you try with His grace supporting you, with divine love and humility as your sources of strength.

If God has planted in your heart the desires to be a doctor, lawyer, pastor, missionary, counselor, business man, teacher, parent, or servant of the poor, go after that dream. But realize that the enemy will try to intimidate you, and lie to you that you are incapable of doing it. If he can hide from you what God wants you to do—the very thing you want to do with all your heart—he will attempt to convince you that you're useless and not intelligent enough to figure it out, let alone succeed at it. But God has put so much into us so that we *can* be of earthly good. What we don't know now, He will teach us, and will put the right people and information in front of us. If our prayer is, "God, just don't let me miss it," He will definitely answer us in ways we can understand. He may not tell us too much ahead of time, but just what we need to know right now, so that we don't get ahead of Him. We can rest assured knowing our life is in God's hands. *I will look to the hills from whence cometh my help; my help cometh from the Lord* (Psalms 121:1).

His Love Perfects Us

People who have accomplished remarkable things have often come from humble beginnings. They knew how things were for them and were determined not to stay there. Some who have not had much will appreciate whatever they are given by God and guard it as their most precious treasure. Not only that, they will take what they have been given and run with it; they will yield a great harvest. They will not be overcome, but shall overcome all obstacles with the love of God:

> *And we know that all things work together for good to them that love God, to them who are the called according to his purpose. For whom he did foreknow, he also did predestinate to be conformed to the image of his Son, that he might be the firstborn among many brethren . . . If God be for us, who can be against us? He that spared not his own Son, but delivered him up for us all, how shall he not with him also freely give us all things? . . . Who shall separate us from the love of Christ? . . . Nay, in all these things, we are more than conquerors through Him that loved us"* (Romans 8:28-29,31-32,35,37).

By choosing to be made into the image and likeness of God's Son, who is love, we acknowledge that there is that in us which has yet to be conformed. By dying with Him, we also rise with

Him in power. We come to esteem only Him and that which comes from Him. What He cannot use in us, we do not want—especially what was in our past:

> *But what things were gain to me, those I counted loss for Christ. Yea doubtless, and I count all things but loss for the excellency of the knowledge of Christ Jesus my Lord: for whom I have suffered the loss of all things, and do count them but dung, that I may win Christ, and be found in him, not having mine own righteousness, which is of the law, but that which is through the faith of Christ. . .That I may know him, and the power of his resurrection, and the fellowship of his sufferings, being made conformable unto his death; if by any means I might attain unto the resurrection of the dead* (Philippians 3:7-11).

A Marriage in the Spirit

God will use our mistakes to make us wiser and better able to serve Him, if we allow Him. By learning what we don't want, He shows us what we do want. Our paths are often circuitous, eventually leading us in the right direction once we have learned what we needed to know. God is bringing us to the right place spiritually, and may give us the right helpmate and even *soul mate* to help us on our journey. There is such a thing as a marriage in the spirit; two people can be of the same mind, heart, and purpose in the spiritual realm, loving each other from that spiritual and personal base. With the crucial element of the Spirit in our relationship, our love will not be merely physical, emotional, sentimental, and fraternal. The Spirit overarches all the other forms of love and perfects them to the level of spiritual union.

Elizabeth Barrett Browning, in her *Sonnets from the Portuguese*, #7 wrote about the beauty and grace of the covenant she viewed as a marriage of souls. According to Browning, the way we see the world becomes forever changed the moment the beloved has come into our life. We are taken from the brink of sinking into "obvious death," have been "caught up into love," and "taught the whole of life in a new rhythm." We find that most difficult circumstances become sweet when braved together. Wherever the beloved is, becomes our home, our country, our world. Everything dear in life takes on new meaning when shared with another who knows us, loves us through and through, and inspires us to believe in God and love Him more intensely than we ever have before.

He Has a Plan

God can give you this surpassing love by which the faith of each catches the other when about to fall. Not only will we pick each other up, we will cause each other to live above the circumstances. God ultimately is behind this love, supporting and encouraging it, for He as our Creator continually supports us in existence and has our best interests at heart. So there is nothing we can't overcome with His love.

Even if you are in a rough family situation where you have children but the children's father or mother has left or died, He can take care of you. Even if you have gotten children before time, and you don't know which way to turn for help, God can redeem that situation. Jesus' mother Mary looked to God her help in a difficult situation (Matthew 1:18-19). While betrothed to Joseph, she was found to be with child. But since God gave Joseph to Mary as the one He had chosen to love and care for her, He would not let Joseph be misled, but directed him to look wisely after her best interests. Once God revealed to Joseph that Mary was carrying the Savior, whom he was to name Jesus, he respected her for what God was doing in her life and how He was using her, and took Mary to be his wife (Matthew 1:20-25).

Every child needs a father, and a loving one at that. He can give those in need of a husband someone like Jesus' foster-father, Joseph, who will love mother and child with God's love, making it seem as if they had always been a family. For Joseph was assumed to be Jesus' natural father (John 6:42), and *was* for all the practical purposes of rearing; he did everything a father did except beget him. Since God picked him out for this special task, he must have put into him all the virtues he'd need. He had to be an extraordinary father, loving and rearing a child that was not his own, simply because that was what God wanted him to do. God must have also given Joseph a tremendous, protective love for Jesus and Mary.

If only all husbands and fathers treated their families with unconditional, self-sacrificing love that would stop at nothing for the sake of their loved ones, all children would want to walk in the will of God. It is important to remember that Joseph was just a distant echo of the eternal Father—everything good about him came from the "Father of mercies," who loves perfectly and gives His children everything they need.

God wants to show us that men and women with the compassionate heart of the Father *do* exist. They are not always born that way, but they are made when people fervently pray, not as much for the right person to *come* into their life, but that they themselves *become* the right person for someone else.

We Will Live in His Love

A union of souls is possible, and that is the experience of love God wants us to have for our spouse. In the beginning, we may have only human love for each other. But if we ask the Lord to give us His heart to love the one He sends us, we will not be disappointed. Divine love for each other grows out of our love for Christ, who causes us to love as He loves. He transforms our love and takes it to another level. His kind of love operates far above the superficial, fickle, recreational variety we see played out by amateurs. God is not kidding around: He takes us seriously as persons: He values us and sees to our needs. We were created to share in His divine life as sons and daughters of God. He is calling for true intimacy with us. When we fully receive Him, He will live in us and we will live in His love:

> *This is the bread which cometh down from heaven, that a man may eat thereof, and not die . . . and the bread that I will give is my flesh, which I give for the life of the world. . . . As the living Father hath sent me, and I live by the Father: so he that eateth me, even he shall live by me* (John 6:50-51,57).

God wants us to experience His divine presence in our lives in a *real* way, and to live continually in *His* love. By reaching out to us with all that He has to give—His very life—He is telling us it is very possible to accept His offer and live out what that offering means. We are to be an offering for God and an offering for each other. In a healthy, loving way, we can even compete with each other in trying to best serve each other's needs. God who is not outdone in generosity will bless our efforts to give of ourselves, because when we do so with a pure heart, we are really giving to Him.

Reach Forth

> *Brethren I count not myself to have apprehended: but this one thing I do, forgetting those things which are behind,* and reaching forth *unto those things which are before, I press toward the mark for the prize of the high calling of God in Christ Jesus* (Philippians 3:13-14, emphasis added).

If we do not see God's hand in events nor hear His guidance, we will tend to grab onto anything—even the first opportunity or person that comes our way—in fear of having nothing or no one. We don't want to be alone, with nothing to hold onto for security. Having something, we are told, is better than nothing, so we make unwise, hasty decisions that lead to painful results. And we are not the only ones who have been hurt. The Lord works with everyone involved to heal the wounds we have helped to bring upon ourselves and others.

With patience, which is wisdom, we can reach forward and press toward the mark, straight as an arrow, hitting the bull's-eye.

We want to be right on target; we have learned what happens when we fall short of, miss, or overshoot the mark. We don't want to go about things the wrong way—spinning our wheels and wasting time, energy, and money. We don't want to feel as if we have no direction or purpose, and are constantly banging up against an unmovable object.

We want to press forward and make progress. God is waiting for us to be willing and He will provide. He wants you to desire His will above all else, and to be hungry for its accomplishment. He is perfecting our will and burning off the dross of selfishness that desires its own ends apart from God. He wants to prepare us as *"a glorious Church, not having spot, or wrinkle, or any such thing; but that it should be holy and without blemish"* (Ephesians 5:27). The effort He makes perfecting us is for our own good, so that we cannot be taken from Him.

> *Let us be glad and rejoice, and give honour to him: for the marriage of the Lamb is come, and his wife hath made herself ready. And to her was granted that she should be arrayed in fine linen, clean and white: for the fine linen is the righteousness of the saints* (Revelations 19:7-8).

You Have to Walk Before You Can Run

His process of perfecting us takes time; we can't handle too much at once. We learn more and more as time goes by to respond to the Spirit's prompting. But there will come times when we feel like we are striving to no avail, as if God has abandoned us. The more I press on, the more opposition I seem to encounter, and the more the situation appears as if God were not in control. It would seem right that life should get easier for us, if we are coming into His presence more often, and we are receiving his peace and direction. But the closer we get to God's will for us, the more the enemy is stirred up to resist us, attempting to make us cease and desist from our activities.

In a sense, God allows us to be proved faithful to His call. We question, "God, where are you?" and He replies, "I'm just trying to perfect you." In Isaiah 40:31, the Word reads, *"For they that wait upon the Lord shall renew their strength."* How can we gain strength if we do not learn to wait? How can we overcome larger obstacles and run longer distances unless we start with smaller ones first? We build endurance with consistent training over a long period of time.

With exercise, we build cardiovascular strength: we breathe easier and do not get cramps nearly as easily as when we first began. Our heart gets stronger, healthier and can pump oxygenated blood to all parts of the body more efficiently in times of need. Then we don't build up as much lactic acid, which causes us to feel sore, though we may still ache on occasion. By persevering in following him, we build up personal and spiritual endurance to press on for Christ, ministering and relating to others in a balanced, loving, life-giving way.

It Will Happen When He Wants

But it is difficult to adjust our thinking in a fast-paced, instant-gratification society such as ours. We want things to come easily. We say, "God, it is now 24 minutes to eight—in two minutes, when I finish praying, I want You to give me the house that I need." Or we pray, "Heal her now, Father, in Jesus' name—*now!*" Does He have to do it in *our* time, how we want it? If He wants to do it now, He will; but do not think you have done it or brought it about more quickly. We can simply pray, "Lord, I claim the house," or "I claim the healing right now, in the name of Jesus, according to Your will." Then we leave it there, freeing Him to act as He sees fit. He is quite capable of healing someone even before you ask.

Bless us, O Lord!

The more of ourselves we give to God—in prayer time, service, witnessing by our actions and encouraging by our words, tithing, and so on—the more God will richly bless us, because we open ourselves to receive, all that He has for us. He wants to pour out the heavens for us; He wants to bless us so that we can barely contain it. We can then spill out our joy upon those who could benefit from it. We can't remember the last time we said to God, "You're blessing me too much. Slow down, Lord; no more right now, please." Rather we thank God for giving us our daily bread; that is enough for us. But if He should sovereignly choose to bless us to overflowing, we won't hold it against Him!

The Greatest of These Is Love

In the end, it doesn't matter how much we have accumulated, known or done. What's important is how much *love* we have put into our endeavors, faith, and acts of charity. We want to be blessed in the area we need it most—the love with which we serve Him together.

> *But covet earnestly the best gifts: and yet show I unto you a more excellent way. . . . And though I have* the gift of *prophesy, and understand all mysteries, and all knowledge; and though I have all faith, so that I could move mountains, and have not charity, I am nothing. And though I bestow all my goods to feed* the poor, *and though I give my body to be burned, and have not charity, it profiteth me nothing. . . .* [Love] *beareth all things, believeth all things, endureth all things. Charity never faileth . . . But when that which is perfect is come, then that which is in part shall be done away. . . . And now abideth faith, hope, and charity, these three; but the greatest of these is charity* (I Corinthians 12:31;13:2-3,7-8,10).